*GREATER THAN A
   ALSO AVAILABL
      AUDIOBOOK FORMAT.

Greater Than a Tourist Book Series Reviews from Readers

I think the series is wonderful and beneficial for tourists to get information before visiting the city.

-Seckin Zumbul, Izmir Turkey

I am a world traveler who has read many trip guides but this one really made a difference for me. I would call it a heartfelt creation of a local guide expert instead of just a guide.

-Susy, Isla Holbox, Mexico

New to the area like me, this is a must have!

 -Joe, Bloomington, USA

This is a good series that gets down to it when looking for things to do at your destination without having to read a novel for just a few ideas.

-Rachel, Monterey, USA

Good information to have to plan my trip to this destination.

-Pennie Farrell, Mexico

Great ideas for a port day.

-Mary Martin USA

Aptly titled, you won't just be a tourist after reading this book. You'll be greater than a tourist!

-Alan Warner, Grand Rapids, USA

Even though I only have three days to spend in San Miguel in an upcoming visit, I will use the author's suggestions to guide some of my time there. An easy read - with chapters named to guide me in directions I want to go.

-Robert Catapano, USA

Great insights from a local perspective! Useful information and a very good value!

-Sarah, USA

This series provides an in-depth experience through the eyes of a local. Reading these series will help you to travel the city in with confidence and it'll make your journey a unique one.

-Andrew Teoh, Ipoh, Malaysia

>TOURIST

GREATER THAN A TOURIST- LAKELAND FLORIDA USA

50 Travel Tips from a Local

Morgan Brownlee

Greater Than a Tourist-Lakeland Florida USA Copyright © 2022 by CZYK Publishing LLC. All Rights Reserved.

All rights reserved. No part of this book may be reproduced in any form or by any electronic or mechanical means including information storage and retrieval systems, without permission in writing from the author. The only exception is by a reviewer, who may quote short excerpts in a review.
This book contains information about establishments where alcohol may be consumed.
The statements in this book are of the authors and may not be the views of CZYK Publishing or Greater Than a Tourist.
First Edition
Cover designed by: Ivana Stamenkovic
Cover Image: https://www.flickr.com/photos/122804914@N05/13746275343/

CZYK Publishing Since 2011.
CZYKPublishing.com
Greater Than a Tourist

Lock Haven, PA
All rights reserved.

ISBN: 9798806266119

>TOURIST

50 TRAVEL TIPS FROM A LOCAL

>TOURIST

BOOK DESCRIPTION

With travel tips and culture in our guidebooks written by a local, it is never too late to visit Lakeland. Greater Than a Tourist- Lakeland, Florida, USA by Author Morgan Brownlee offers the inside scoop on Lakeland, Florida and all there is to this little gem in the Sunshine State. Most travel books tell you how to travel like a tourist. Although there is nothing wrong with that, as part of the 'Greater Than a Tourist' series, this book will give you candid travel tips from someone who has lived at your next travel destination. This guide book will not tell you exact addresses or store hours but instead gives you knowledge that you may not find in other smaller print travel books. Experience cultural, culinary delights, and attractions with the guidance of a Local. Slow down and get to know the people with this invaluable guide. By the time you finish this book, you will be eager and prepared to discover new activities at your next travel destination.

Inside this travel guide book you will find:

- Visitor information from a Local
- Tour ideas and inspiration
- Valuable guidebook information

Greater Than a Tourist- A Travel Guidebook with 50 Travel Tips from a Local. Slow down, stay in one place, and get to know the people and culture. By the time you finish this book, you will be eager and prepared to travel to your next destination.

OUR STORY

Traveling is a passion of the Greater than a Tourist book series creator. Lisa studied abroad in college, and for their honeymoon Lisa and her husband toured Europe. During her travels to Malta, an older man tried to give her some advice based on his own experience living on the island since he was a young boy. She was not sure if she should talk to the stranger but was interested in his advice. When traveling to some places she was wary to talk to locals because she was afraid that they weren't being genuine. Through her travels, Lisa learned how much locals had to share with tourists. Lisa created the Greater Than a Tourist book series to help connect people with locals. A topic that locals are very passionate about sharing.

TABLE OF CONTENTS

Book Description
Our Story
Table of Contents
Dedication
About the Author
How to Use This Book
From the Publisher
WELCOME TO > TOURIST
1. Born and Bread Bakery
2. Lake Morton Royal Avians
3. Swan Brewing
4. Cob and Pen
5. Pressed Bookstore and Coffee Shop
6. Union Hall
7. Joker Marchant Stadium (Publix Field)
8. Bryant Stadium and the Dreadnaughts
9. Southeastern University
10. Florida Southern College Architecture
11. Lake Hollingsworth
12. Circle B Bar Reserve
13. The Balance Culture
14. Concord Coffee
15. Ax-Caliber Ax Venue and Coffee House
16. Nineteen61

17. Red Door Lakeland
18. The Joinery
19. Cafe Zuppina
20. Downtown Food Truck Rally and *The Squeeze*
21. Brunch at the Terrace Hotel
22. Revival Cocktail Bar
23. Munn Park
24. Downtown Shops
25. First Friday
26. Downtown Farmer's Market
27. Parkesdale Farm Market
28. Keel & Curley Winery
29. Florida Strawberry Festival
30. Common Ground Playground
31. Cleveland Heights Golf Course
32. Eaglebrooke Golf Club
33. Freshwater Fishing
34. Peterson Park
35. Tea Largo and Picassoz
36. Colt Creek State Park
37. Hollis Gardens on Lake Mirror
38. Shopping at Lakeside Village
39. Daydreams Day Spa
40. Polk Museum of Art
41. Sun 'n Fun
42. Polk Theatre

43. Silvermoon Drive-In Theatre
44. DEFY Lakeland
45. Bok Tower Gardens
46. Legoland
47. RP Funding Center
48. Lakeland Magic
49. Explorations V Children's Museum
50. The Poor Porker

TOP REASONS TO BOOK THIS TRIP:

Other Resources:

Packing and Planning Tips

Travel Questions

Travel Bucket List

NOTES

\>TOURIST

DEDICATION

This book is dedicated to my husband Zach, whom I met and fell in love with in this fantastic little city.

>TOURIST

ABOUT THE AUTHOR

Morgan is a high school English teacher who lives in Lakeland, Florida, where she lives with her husband Zach and their two pets who they spoil rotten: Luna the boxer mix and Cece the Ragdoll cat.

Morgan loves to cook (and eat), drink good wine, and read books by the many lakes in Lakeland. She also loves to travel and her favorite places in the world are Mount Rainier in Washington state and the Swiss Alps.

Morgan settled in Lakeland after attending college there for 4 years. The city always felt more like home than the one she grew up in. When she met and fell in love with her husband here, they decided it was the place to stay. They love the quiet of the smaller city with the benefits of the world's best theme parks and beaches just a few miles away.

If you want to follow more of Morgan's life–and by life we mean the food she eats and the places she travels to–you can follow her public Instagram @eats_by_morgan. She will also answer any and all questions about Lakeland that you may be left with!

HOW TO USE THIS BOOK

The *Greater Than a Tourist* book series was written by someone who has lived in an area for over three months. The goal of this book is to help travelers either dream or experience different locations by providing opinions from a local. The author has made suggestions based on their own experiences. Please check before traveling to the area in case the suggested places are unavailable.

Travel Advisories: As a first step in planning any trip abroad, check the Travel Advisories for your intended destination.
https://travel.state.gov/content/travel/en/traveladvisories/traveladvisories.html

FROM THE PUBLISHER

Traveling can be one of the most important parts of a person's life. The anticipation and memories that you have are some of the best. As a publisher of the Greater Than a Tourist, as well as the popular *50 Things to Know* book series, we strive to help you learn about new places, spark your imagination, and inspire you. Wherever you are and whatever you do I wish you safe, fun, and inspiring travel.

Lisa Rusczyk Ed. D.
CZYK Publishing

>TOURIST

```
WELCOME TO
> TOURIST
```

>TOURIST

*""We travel not to escape life
but for life not to escape us."*

- Robyn Yong

Lakeland, Florida, is a city that many thousands of tourists will visit each year without really realizing they have visited it. This is because it exists perfectly on the famous I-4, the state road in Florida that connects the Atlantic Ocean with the Gulf of Mexico. Busy travelers adorned with Mickey Mouse ears or beach towels will breeze right through, missing the entirety of the beauty that is found in the central Florida city. While there's certainly the obvious attractions like Disney World and Clearwater Beach, both of which are only a 40-50 minute drive from Lakeland, we will be further scoping out all the unique small businesses, nature preserves, and local events that make Lakeland one of the fastest growing cities in the United States (according to 2019-2020 Census data).

When I first moved to Lakeland in 2014, I didn't expect to stay. I was from Pittsburgh, Pennsylvania. I was accustomed to overcast skies, fast-paced environments, and mountains. While I still have a love for the mountains, I quickly found my homesickness was easily cured by a trip to the beach with a good book. I got used to seeing a bluebird sky nearly everyday, and after surviving my first hurricane, I realized I could do this. When I graduated from college in 2018, I found myself looking for reasons to stay. What was once foreign was now home. I took a job at the local city high school, met and fell in love with my husband (a fellow teacher), and have called Lakeland home ever since. I never expected to love it, and you probably don't either. But you will. My parents and one of my sisters have even moved down since I did because their vacations here just weren't enough anymore. This little city will capture your heart with its kindness, closeness, and southern charm.

Lakeland definitely has a small-town feel, comparable to Charleston, South Carolina, or Savannah, Georgia. It makes a perfect long weekend getaway, especially when you're looking to escape a bigger city, but you still want the conveniences of city life. Lakeland will help you slow down, eat well, and feel at home, getting you rested and rejuvenated. It has just the right amount of events and nightlife to keep you up and going with outings and all of the accommodations and opportunities to lay by stunning

>TOURIST

lakes or take a quick trip to the beach. Whatever you want to do, Lakeland can help you do it. The best part of all? You will be hard-pressed to find a city with better food while you take on whatever you choose.

So here we go! These are just some of the reasons why you should visit Lakeland, Florida, on your next trip to the fabulous and tropical Sunshine State.

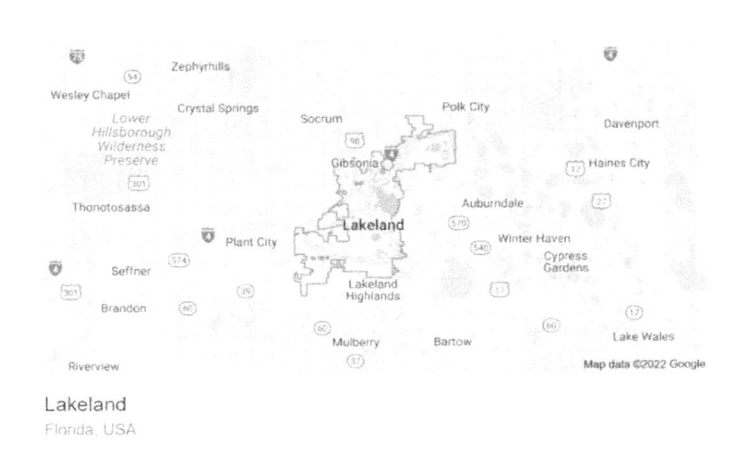

Lakeland
Florida, USA

Lakeland Florida Climate

	High	Low
January	71	51
February	74	53
March	79	57
April	83	62
May	88	67
June	91	72
July	91	74
August	91	74
September	89	73
October	84	67
November	78	59
December	73	54

GreaterThanaTourist.com

Temperatures are in Fahrenheit degrees.
Source: NOAA

>TOURIST

1. BORN AND BREAD BAKERY

This is my favorite place in all of Lakeland. This bakery and its owner, Jennifer Smurr, have been recognized by *Forbes* magazine for its success. Home to the uniquely named and delicious cruffin–a croissant muffin–this bakery has become a must-see pitstop for many foodie travelers. I have been all over the world and I must say, this bakery is the best I've ever been to. Their croissants are the size of your face, and their breakfast sandwiches are made from the freshest ingredients. Every single pastry you receive will look exactly like the ones they post pictures of on Instagram. They're a little piece of art that tastes as good (if not better) as it looks.

As of now it is only open on Wednesday and Saturday mornings. You'll have to check their website for their daily menu and hours. I recommend ordering ahead online, but you don't have to. If you don't order ahead and the line is long, just wait in it. It moves quickly, and more than that, it's totally worth it. Trust me, if you do nothing else on this list, you have to grab a pastry and a locally-roasted cold brew from Born and Bread.

2. LAKE MORTON ROYAL AVIANS

Yes, we do have a lot of lakes in Lakeland. We also have a lot of swans. We are obsessed with these swans. In 1953 Queen Elizabeth herself heard that Lakeland was looking for swans, so she donated 2 out of her personal flock. All the city had to do was pay for shipping! The swan population is now thriving, and most of them choose to swim in the beautiful Lake Morton.

If you're lucky, you may even get to see the Annual Swan Roundup where local veterinarians check in on the health of the swan community. This usually takes place in October. The swans are literally rounded up and brought out of the lakes and local officials hold them gently in their laps while the vets check their vitals. There's just nothing quite like watching your mayor pet the neck of a swan while it gets its heart checked. Only in Lakeland!

Even if you don't stop, chances are good that you'll drive past Lake Morton. We do ask that you drive carefully. As I've mentioned, we really do love

>TOURIST

our swans and if one gets hurt, the entire community hurts with it. If you decide to get out to see them, please do not try to touch them as they are wild animals. You can also feed them, but it's suggested you toss whole grains, such as wheat, and vegetable matter, especially lettuce and potatoes, into the water for them. Please avoid rice, bread, and sugar. We want our royal avians to stay healthy for their next check up, and we thank you for respecting this!

3. SWAN BREWING

Once you are done watching the swans, you can head over to Swan Brewing, a local establishment that often features live music and food trucks. While it's family and pet friendly, you must be 21+ to enjoy the local and craft brews they offer. Play some darts, listen to the live entertainment, and join in on a friendly game of corn hole as you relax by Lake Wire under the shady, breezy tent.

Some of their brews that I enjoy most include: *Straight Outta Lakeland* which is an IPA and is brewed right there at Swan; the *Freedom* brew, another Swan masterpiece and gold-medal winner,

17

and any of the Ciderboys ciders they happen to have when you stop in! The menu changes often, so feel free to check their website or Instagram before you go.

4. COB AND PEN

Another Swan City establishment is Cob and Pen (the names for male and female swans). This restaurant is unique because the 1927 Tudor house once sat about a mile away in a local historic neighborhood called Dixieland. In 2016 they loaded the house on a flatbed truck and drove it to its current location on South Florida Avenue. Pets are welcome on the patio and lawn, and there's corn hole for the kids (or kids at heart). The unique pub-style menu features local brews and wines, as well as craft cocktails. If you go on a Monday, prepare for an intense round of trivia with the locals, and check their specials board because they often give discounts to college students, first responders, and teachers. They also have a small quick-serve restaurant located down the street called *Good Thyme*, which is open for breakfast and lunch daily Monday-Friday.

>TOURIST

One more interesting thing about Cob and Pen? They feature local art from prominent Lakeland artists, such as Jason DeMeo. The art is available for purchase and changes every now and then. They also have large projector screens for local sporting events, as well as private dining options.

5. PRESSED BOOKSTORE AND COFFEE SHOP

Who doesn't love a good read on vacation? While you can hit up the big chains beforehand, if you forget or if you're feeling extra whimsical, you can stop by the new downtown bookstore, *Pressed*. It also has free Wifi and comfy seating, so it's also the perfect place to catch up on some emails (if you're the work-from-vacation type). The locally roasted coffee from Ethos Roasters is smooth, the pastries from the local bakery–Honeycomb–are sweet, and the overall experience is unmatched..

Not only does *Pressed* have all the newest and most popular releases, it also features books by local authors. *Goodnight, Lakeland* is one popular children's book by local author Ida Mundell and local artist Josh "Bump" Galletta. If you're bringing the kids, there is also free story reading at 9:30 am every Wednesday! You can also find local art and photography for sale on the walls.

6. UNION HALL

Union Hall is a local bar and live music venue. It often hosts holiday-themed parties and concerts for a very low fee. If you love small-venue concerts or shows, this place is for you. Union Hall also often features unique eats from local food trucks. This can be a great way to end the evening, just make sure you check their schedule ahead of time to see who is playing!

The building itself, like most others in the area, is historic. It was built in 1920 and the interior of the building focuses on the beautiful exposed brick. This venue is also popular for weddings and other events. It may not look like much from the outside, but it really is a beautiful place to go, especially if you love old architecture.

>TOURIST

7. JOKER MARCHANT STADIUM (PUBLIX FIELD)

Calling all baseball fans! This one's for you! Lakeland is home to the longest-standing Spring Break relationship in MLB history with the Detroit Tigers. The Tiger's began their preseason practice games in Lakeland in 1927, and they've been at Joker Marchant Stadium since 1966.

If you come in the spring, you may get to catch a game. Tickets are priced low and there's not a bad seat in the house. If you are here in the summer, you can still see the Flying Tigers play. They also often feature special nights, like the 4th of July fireworks and other family-friendly events to get you outside and enjoying America's favorite pastime.

8. BRYANT STADIUM AND THE DREADNAUGHTS

Baseball not your thing? That's fine, because Lakeland also happens to be home to one of the most premier public high school football teams, the Lakeland Dreadnaughts. While it may not be your first go-to for a vacation event, Lakeland football is next-level. With players like the Pouncey twins who played in the NFL and countless other Division I recruits out of LHS each year, you never know if you're witnessing the next G.O.A.T. They also play at historic Bryant Stadium and Bill Castle Field.

LHS football is often referred to as the Gainesville Pipeline because so many players have gone on to play at the University of Florida. If you're a mega sports buff, have a love for up-and-coming SEC stars, or just a fan of some good hometown nostalgia, this is one you don't want to miss. Like I said, you may just be watching the start of football's next big thing.

>TOURIST

9. SOUTHEASTERN UNIVERSITY

Need to get a quick college visit while you're here? Southeastern University, the largest Christian University in the US when you consider the online and branch campus locations, is based in Lakeland and is home to the NAIA Championship Fire Baseball Team. SEU also has football, basketball, wrestling, soccer, and more. In addition to their sports, they have a worship team that has albums available on all streaming services, such as Spotify and Apple Music.

Regarding academics, the school offers degrees ranging from A.A's and Bachelor's programs to Doctoral and PhD programs. They have everything from nursing and pre-med, to graphic design, music business, and more. The small school environment is often preferred by students who like to have the teachers know their name. The campus is stunning, dawning a Spanish-type architectural design throughout. Cobblestone sidewalks, palm trees, and fountains can be found throughout the school grounds as music plays softly through hidden speakers. It's a great stop if you're on the hunt for a private, religiously affiliated university, or if you just need a short walk to stretch your legs!

10. FLORIDA SOUTHERN COLLEGE ARCHITECTURE

The other major school located in the heart of Lakeland is Florida Southern College. While it is smaller than Southeastern (which can certainly be part of the draw), it does boast a major claim to fame as its campus was designed by world renowned architect and artist, Frank Lloyd Wright. Also known for his home, Fallingwater, and the Gugenheim in New York City, Frank Lloyd Wright's campus can be seen sitting on the glistening waters of Lake Hollingsworth. Visitors can request a free campus tour, or guide themselves along the beautiful sidewalks of FSC. Be sure to stop by the rose garden and the Water Dome fountain!

In addition to the stunning architecture, FSC also has phenomenal academics and Greek life. Students can experience a private education with a public feel. Unlike neighboring SEU, they don't have a football

>TOURIST

team, so you may want to learn the rules for lacrosse or baseball! Whether you're interested in the school as a place to learn or a place to admire a famous artist's work

11. LAKE HOLLINGSWORTH

Yes, another lake. This one is at the center of Lakeland itself and proudly boasts some of the most magnificent sunsets in the city. Hollingsworth is often the host of water skiing shows and large outdoor events. You can often find Yoga by the Lake or rollerblading groups zipping along its nearly perfect 3-mile radius. Florida Southern College sits on one end of it, while the Lakeland Country Club sits on the other. Surrounded by stunning homes with impeccable landscaping, Hollingsworth is a community staple to walk around. Just keep your eyes peeled for the local wildlife. From alligators to otters, Hollingsworth is full of valuable Florida ecosystems.

My favorite time to walk or drive around Hollingsworth are the holidays. Most of the houses feature professional lighting and decor and it's beautiful. You really haven't experienced the holidays until you see palm trees wrapped in lights! You can also hang around the stunning Lake Hollingsworth Presbyterian Church to wait for the hourly church bells.

If you're brave enough to get in the water (I admittedly am not, but many people do every day), you can also kayak, jet ski, or boat here. We see people water skiing and tubing all the time, and there is also a really cool motorcycle/jet ski hybrid that can be seen going straight from Hollingsworth Road to Hollingsworth Lake. You really never know what Floridians will come up with, but this invention is really cool.

>TOURIST
12. CIRCLE B BAR RESERVE

Were the alligators at the city lakes too shy for you? Don't worry! We have more! Circle B Bar Reserve is one of the best places to go to spot the prehistoric giants. There's even a trail called Alligator Alley that they have to close during mating season. Bobcats, wild boar, bald eagles, tropical birds, tortoises, and even a Florida Panther also call this place home. It is because of all the wildlife that you are not permitted to bring pets to Circle B. Trust me… you want to leave your furry friends home for this one.

This is my husband's favorite place to hike. Personally I'm terrified of alligators, so when we go we take the Shady Oak Trail or the Eagle Roost. But once a year on his birthday, I brave the trek through Alligator Alley. Don't get me wrong–it's the best trail they have. Just go with your courage in-hand because they are seriously everywhere. To give you a point of reference, if you remember the viral video of the monster alligator walking across a hiker's path from 2017… that was at Circle B Bar Reserve.

13. THE BALANCE CULTURE

Not in the mood for a hike? You can still find amazing ways to work out your body while you're visiting Lakeland! My personal favorite is just for the ladies. The Balance Culture is an all women's fitness studio that offers classes such as barre, spin, yoga, pilates, spin, weight training, and more.

My favorite class is definitely Pilates. Created by Joseph Pilates for soldiers returning from war and professional dancers, it has some really great stretching and the core work is just challenging enough to feel it the next day, but I don't usually break out in a heavy sweat. It's the perfect place to workout, feel super encouraged, and start (or end) your day well. It's also fantastic for some girl time because like I said: no boys allowed. Oh, and if you're nervous to pay to try something new–don't worry! Your first class is free!

If you can't make it to the Balance Culture because of class times that don't match your itinerary, or because you're not a woman, then you can also check out the local All-American gym, an old-fashioned workout facility near downtown, or the chain gyms such as Gold's Gym, AnyTime Fitness, or Planet Fitness, all of which have Lakeland locations.

14. CONCORD COFFEE

After you break a sweat or wait for the women in your life to finish their fitness class, head over to a local staple–Concord Coffee. This location is one of only 2, and their own roastery is right next door. The other location is in Gainesville, Florida, on the University of Florida campus. Pastries from various local bakeries, such as Honeycomb Bakery in Lakeland, are on the menu at both locations. I would highly recommend the vanilla latte, iced or hot!

Other coffee houses in Lakeland that I would recommend are: Mitchell's, Black and Brew (downtown or library location), Pressed, and Hillcrest. All of these shops have locally roasted and ethically sourced coffee beans. I'd say skip Starbucks and Dunkin' on this trip altogether. You really don't need it here because they're no comparison to what our residents have created. Not to mention the local pastries all of them serve that the chains just can't compete with.

15. AX-CALIBER AX VENUE AND COFFEE HOUSE

If you need to blow off some steam, entertain kids, and have a cup of coffee, head over to Ax-Caliber! Ax-Caliber is Lakeland's local ax-throwing cafe. We love a good cup of coffee here, and people have definitely gotten creative with tempting you to try theirs. Ax-caliber also has a full menu, so you might as well stay for dinner. This family-friendly downtown location is a must-do. Check their website for weekly offers and to make reservations. If you don't reserve your time, you may have to wait a little bit. If that doesn't bother you then feel free to just drop in!

16. NINETEEN61

If you're looking for a dinner spot that's a little more formal or romantic, look no further than Nineteen61. This downtown local spot is a go-to for all your fine dining desires. The modern Latin cuisine is second to none, and the wine and cocktail menu is extensive. The interior exposed brick shows off the historic nature of the building and guests are guaranteed an intimate and delicious dinner. My go-to is always the Ropa Vieja and I finish it off with the guayaba cheesecake and a café con leche!

If you have a really large group, you can also look into renting their rooftop. This requires a minimum guest count of 10, and more information can be requested by filling out their contact form on their website. This may also be dependent on the time of year, but the view definitely makes reaching out worth the effort.

17. RED DOOR LAKELAND

If you are looking for a restaurant with a menu that changes seasonally and a wine list to make you drool, Red Door is where you want to go! Their owner, Richard DeAngellis, often floats the intimate dining room and front porch to mingle with his guests and offer suggestions. It's a wonderfully personal dining experience, and the food itself is a foodie's dream. I have to say, I have had a lot of Key Lime pie living in this state… Red Door is the best I've ever had (sorry Key West). My favorite menu item for dinner that they've ever had was a smoked pork loin with the juices reinjected in order to elevate the meat's tenderness. It was served with a phenomenal blend of root veggies and a red pepper sauce that I still dream about. We love Red Door so much we had our rehearsal dinner on their patio! When you go, feel free to park across the street at the public library and art museum!

>TOURIST

18. THE JOINERY

If you have kids or a diverse group, you may want to try out The Joinery! Located in downtown Lakeland, The Joinery is a modern food hall that boasts a full bar and multiple cuisines. From ramen to barbeque to cheeseburgers, The Joinery has something for everyone to love. And no matter which restaurant you choose to eat at, you can all wrap up the meal with a flight of fresh ice cream from Mayday.

The Joinery also happens to have a fabulous floral shop in it, Bloomshakalaka. The florists there create "funky, fresh" arrangements in addition to the local ceramic vases and candles they sell. It's a great place to grab something to brighten up your hotel room or AirBnB!

Parking can be a bit of an issue because this venue is so popular with tourists and locals. If you can't find parking in their lot, you can park in the street spots around Lake Mirror, or just up the street there's another lot under the overpass.

19. CAFE ZUPPINA

If you're looking for a hole in the wall that will absolutely blow your mind, look no further than Cafe Zuppina. One of my absolute favorite local spots, Cafe Zuppina is a Turkish-Mediterranean restaurant and bakery. For such an obscure location, they have vegetarian options that will blow your mind, as well as traditional meals for meat lovers. The bakery has gluten-free and vegan pastries as well as everything in between. The best part? It's all made fresh from imported ingredients by one lady and a pastry chef. It's life changing. It will make the Mediterranean stop in Epcot feel second-rate because this one little cafe blows it away.

Cafe Zuppina also has a Mediterranean market attached to it. It sells delicious to-go style soups, salads, and dips, as well as fresh ingredients for you to cook with at home. Be sure to try the feta cheese from the Marketplace and, of course, the hummus. No trip to a Mediterranean shop is complete without trying the hummus.

20. DOWNTOWN FOOD TRUCK RALLY AND *THE SQUEEZE*

If you haven't noticed, food is pretty big in Lakeland. For a small city, we have a lot of meal options. If you happen to be in town on the third Thursday of the month, head to Munn Park for the Downtown Food Truck Rally. There you'll find an array of food, from Mexican to burgers to a French crepe truck. It's a great way to get out and have a whole new culinary experience. Bring a chair and a blanket, though! A lot of people turn out for this one, so Munn Park runs out of seating pretty quickly.

I suggest parking in one of the Lakeland parking garages. They're free on weekdays after 5:00 pm and on weekends! You can also park on the street and find a local stop for *The Squeeze*. These professionally driven golf carts are a small city solution to its epic recent growth. Just wait at the station (as far away as Florida Southern or RP Funding), pay on the app or via cash, and ride! You can download the Citrus Connection mPass to pay virtually. The rates can be found on Citrus Connect's website, but they range between $0.75 (seniors) to $1.50. Kids under 7 ride free.

21. BRUNCH AT THE TERRACE HOTEL

We've talked a lot about dinner, but we do brunch really well, too. The Terrace Hotel is definitely the crème de la crème of brunches in Lakeland. The historic hotel just had a big facelift during its 2021 renovation and is officially back open and ready to wow you. With picturesque views of Lake Mirror and fabulous wait staff, you can't go wrong brunching here. While you're at it, you might as well just book a room so you can brunch again the next day!

The menu can be a little pricey, so you may want to check it out before you book a reservation. My choice is the Terrace Frittata, which is currently listed at $14.00. Parking can be found on the street all over downtown, or in the parking garage across the street from the hotel!

>TOURIST
22. REVIVAL COCKTAIL BAR

If you're looking for a nightcap, look no further than Revival. My favorite bar in town, Revival is a relaxed cocktail bar that features unique concoctions as well as traditional ones. It's a great place to meet up with friends because the environment, while fun and laid back, also feels mature and professional. Locals tend to go for Friday cocktails, while tourists come in on various nights of the week for fruity Tiki drinks and creative mixes you can't get anywhere else. You can even come by yourself, grab a book from the book wall, and post up with no questions or judgements. The only rules (as told to me by the owner once) are no kids, no pets, and no smoking.

As far as drink recommendations go, my husband would tell you to get the Duck Fat Old Fashioned, while I tend to go for the Once and Floral or a traditional gimlet. I also love to try their weekly Revival. They recently had a strawberry rhubarb drink that was so good I went back the next day to have it again. You can check their Instagram to see what the Weekly Revival is, or just stop by and ask. Either way, it's probably worth a try!

23. MUNN PARK

Florida's obvious claim-to-fame is our fabulous weather. We have nearly perfect temperatures year round. In the spring and the fall I love nothing more than grabbing a blanket and a book and heading outdoors to bask in the sunshine. Munn Park is at the center of downtown. While it's nothing fancy, it does have grassy areas for kids to play and is surrounded by amazing cafes to grab to-go style for a picnic. I always love to stop into Black and Brew for a sandwich and an iced coffee before sitting in the park and enjoying it.

24. DOWNTOWN SHOPS

If you haven't realized, Lakeland is a small-business owner's dream and we are insanely proud of the creative talent who live here. The downtown shops are almost all locally owned and operated.

Some of my favorite downtown shops are Scout and Tag and Rafa Naturals. Scout and Tag offers home goods while Rafa Naturals has homemade soaps, all-natural cleaners, and other scented cleaning and body products. They are both such fun places to browse in, as are all the other little places you can find! There's also a fun shop called Top Buttons. Top Buttons is a second hand clothing store and nonprofit organization that benefits girls in need within the community. The clothing selection is fashion-forward, a mix of new and used, and reasonably priced.

25. FIRST FRIDAY

The downtown area really gets going on the first Friday of every month, creatively dubbed "First Friday". This is when local businesses, classic car owners, schools, talents, and more all come out for a themed evening on the town together. It's family-friendly, stores stay open late, and there's always something new to do at it. Some of the themes that are up-and-coming are: Spring Fling (April 2022), Family Fun Night (May 2022), Bike Night by Harley Davidson (July 2022), and Cookie Carnival (October 2022), among others! Just check out Downtown Lakeland's website to find what the theme is during your visit.

26. DOWNTOWN FARMER'S MARKET

Every city needs a farmer's market, and Lakeland's is one of the best. One of the privileges of being in the south is there is always fresh produce available. The springtime is the best for strawberries, while the summer has amazing watermelon. Farmer's market goers can also find food trucks with different local cuisines, ranging from fresh Cuban food to French crepes and coffee. Plants, clothing, and locally curated goods are all for sale at this large outdoor market space.

Of all the stands, my favorite to stop at is Red Roof Farms Honey. It's veteran owned and operated. While you may not be able to reap the allergen benefits as a tourist, the Orange Blossom Honey is sure to be a crowd pleaser on your next charcuterie tray wherever home is for you! It may be important to note that this honey is not FDA approved.

>TOURIST

27. PARKESDALE FARM MARKET

If you're willing to drive just a bit outside of the city of Lakeland, you can go to a market that's open more frequently, the Parkesdale Market in Plant City. In addition to the farmer's market goods, this market is known for its strawberry shortcake. It really is amazing, and they'll load it up with local Florida strawberries. If you're trying to avoid the carbs, you can even order a bowl of just the strawberries and whipped topping.

While I do love a good strawberry shortcake, I actually enjoy their strawberry milkshake even more. The fruit is fresh and it makes all the difference. It's creamy and cold and let's face it: sometimes Florida is way too hot and we all need a sweet way to cool off.

28. KEEL & CURLEY WINERY

While central Florida will never be Napa Valley, we do pretty well with our sweet fruit wines! Keel & Curley is the place to go for your winery needs. Located just off I-4 as you're headed out of Lakeland toward Tampa, it's impossible to miss. When you stop at the winery, make sure you try the Sangria and the Key Lime wine.

During strawberry season you can participate in U-Pick which will result in you having a ton of fresh Florida strawberries. If you happened to drive to Lakeland for your trip, buy as many as you want. But even if you flew here, as long as you aren't going to Hawaii or another country you can take home your berries (and any other fresh Florida produce, such as oranges) as a carry-on or personal item. Once you get them home, you can make amazing jams, pies, or other desserts with them. You can also, of course, just eat them fresh. I find my fresh berries to be best 1-2 days after we've picked them.

>TOURIST

29. FLORIDA STRAWBERRY FESTIVAL

If you're anywhere near the Lakeland/Plant City area in the month of March, make sure you check to see if you are able to go to the Strawberry Festival! With all things strawberries, fair rides, and free music from top artists (tickets for closer seats can be purchased, but it's not necessary), the Strawberry Festival is not something you want to miss out on.

The 2022 Strawberry Festival featured artists such as Cole Swindell, Sam Hunt, Lauren Daigle, and more. Artists for each year's festival aren't released until a few months before, so you will need to check their website to see who is going to be there. You'll also want to make sure you stop by Peachy's donut truck. Oh, and bring cash! Some vendors are only able to take cash at the fair.

Finally, if you plan on going to the Strawberry Festival you should buy a ticket ahead of time at a nearby Publix. Not only is the cost reduced, you will also eliminate having to wait a very long time in a very long line. Parking is usually cash only and can fill up, so come early or come prepared to walk a bit. They always expect big crowds, so it's not impossible to find a place but it's always good to know what you are getting into!

30. COMMON GROUND PLAYGROUND

Bringing kids on a vacation can sometimes make it seem like it's not a vacation. Common Ground can help entertain them and get some of those travel jitters out. Best of all? It was designed for children of all abilities in mind, so every child is able to join in on the fun. Your kids will have a great time and they'll learn inclusivity at the same time. It is incredibly well-maintained by the city and is located right by Lake Hollingsworth and Cleveland Heights Golf Course.

>TOURIST

31. CLEVELAND HEIGHTS GOLF COURSE

Golfing in Florida is always prime, and the Cleveland Heights Golf Course is a lower-cost way to get a round in. This public golf course has a Pro-shop, golf lessons, and a full service restaurant inside. Play for nine or all eighteen, either way you're sure to have a good time for a lower price. Make sure you book your tee time a day or so before you go if you come during high-tourist times, like the holidays and the spring, though they usually have openings available year-round.

32. EAGLEBROOKE GOLF CLUB

If you want a more private, upscale golf experience, I would suggest Eaglebrooke. It's located within a gated residency, but anyone can play there for a fee. Their beautiful clubhouse has a Pro-shop and a full-service restaurant. You can also host events there even if you're not a member. I actually had my wedding at this course and it was phenomenal. The food, the drinks, the staff, and, of course, the greens are all amazing, and it remains one of Lakeland's highest rated golf courses with public access. If you've got a non-golfer, you can ask about purchasing a day-pass or seasonal pass to their pool and tennis courts.

33. FRESHWATER FISHING

If the gators don't scare you, you may want to try your hand at fishing in one of Lakeland's many lakes. This is a perk of a small city as there are many quiet spots to wet a line. In addition to largemouth bass, you might also catch channel catfish, redear sunfish, black crappie, bluegill, chain pickerel, peacock bass, and sunshine bass.

If you decide you want to fish while you're visiting and you're over the age of 16, make sure you obtain a fishing license from the Florida Fish and Wildlife Conservation Commission. There's a free Fish | Hunt Florida app that can help you with this, or you can visit their website. A visitor's freshwater permit for 3 days costs $17.00, or you can get a Gone Fishing annual pass that covers all freshwater and saltwater fishing with lobster and snook permits for $114, and that includes the cost of a hard card displaying your license. It really comes down to how much you want to fish, where you want to fish, and how long you'll be in Florida!

34. PETERSON PARK

Another picture-esque park in our city is Peterson Park. This one has beautiful wooden bridges and landscaping that is often favored by photographers. It also has baseball fields and a playground that are available for public use. Bring a camera, hang a hammock, and enjoy!

If you want to get really into it, you can book a session with a local photographer to memorialize your stay in central Florida. The shade from the massive oaks and the southern elegance of the Spanish moss is sure to help capture the most aesthetic family photos you'll ever get.

35. TEA LARGO AND PICASSOZ

These experiences go hand-in-hand! Grab an acai bowl or bubble tea from Tea Largo before heading over to the local ceramics studio, Picassoz, to create your next masterpiece. They;re known for their unique mosaics, which you can take home with you that day. You'll leave refreshed physically and mentally from this one! This is also a great place to go if you get a wet weekend or if the summer air is just too hot for you to handle.

As far as Tea Largo goes, if you've never tried an acai bowl I highly suggest it. I like to top mine with regular granola, honey, mango, strawberries, bananas, and the vegan chocolate chips. When it's chilly or raining out, I stop in for a vanilla chai latte. No matter what you get, your body and your taste buds will thank you for the deliciously healthy snack.

36. COLT CREEK STATE PARK

This particular park is the best if you have a love for biking, with over 12 miles of trail available to bikers and hikers. It's a pet friendly park, so feel free to bring your furry friend! Just make sure you also bring a least as pets are required to be on one at all times.

You can also camp at Colt Creek in a tent or a camper, but make sure to reserve your spot ahead of time. They have full hookups on limited spots, as well as tent lots. If you like to go really off-the-grid, they also have a primitive camping lot where you can really set up to rough it. They are also able to accommodate horse trailers for trail riders! How many other cities can say that?

37. HOLLIS GARDENS ON LAKE MIRROR

A walk around downtown's Lake Mirror isn't complete without a stroll through the beautiful Hollis Gardens. Just a short walk from The Joinery, Hollis Gardens is a piece of serenity right in the middle of the city. With 1.2 acres of over 10,000 blooms and greenery, you're sure to come across something you find breathtaking. Definitely bring a camera (or just your phone). If you're lucky, you may even get to see a proposal as this is a popular spot to pop the question. I got engaged there, myself!

You never know what major life moment you may come across here, but even if you don't get that little thrill you can still feel your blood pressure lowering as you take in the stunning blooms and foliage of the Gardens. Note that Hollis Gardens is always closed on Mondays, no matter the season.

38. SHOPPING AT LAKESIDE VILLAGE

If you love to shop, you may want to stop by Lakeside Village! Home to boutiques like Francesca's and high-end diamond stores like the International Diamond Center, you are sure to find something you love. Restaurants and bars also dot this upscale, outdoor shopping center. You can find everything from chains like Olive Garden, Longhorn, and Abuelo's, to more local places like Thai Oshi. Lakeside Village also has a large, modern movie theater, CMX Cinemas Lakeside 18 & IMAX (formerly and more locally referred to as the Cobb). Here you can find everything new and current in theaters. During the holidays the center square of the Village has a massive Christmas tree and pictures with Santa (for free).

39. DAYDREAMS DAY SPA

Once you shop til you drop at Lakeside Village, step into the cool, relaxing environment of Daydreams Day Spa. Shop for some rejuvenating products (I like Farmhouse Fresh), or schedule a deep-tissue massage, facial, manicure, pedicure, or more. We often go to Daydreams for a couple's massage just to work out the stresses of our daily lives.

My favorite way to unwind on any vacation is to start my trip with a massage. If you've never tried that approach, it's a definite game changer. If you come to Lakeland looking to unwind and relax, Daydreams is the place to go. It's more affordable than the big spas at the resorts in Tampa and Orlando, but don't let that convince you that it's not amazing, because it is. They also offer custom packages. Call the spa to reserve your desired services!

>TOURIST
40. POLK MUSEUM OF ART

Lakeland loves three things: swans, food/drink, and art. The Polk Museum of Art is a fabulous way to spend an afternoon, especially if it's hot or raining (which is often in our tropical climate). Founded in 1966, it has slowly grown to be "the largest and only nationally accredited visual arts organization in Polk County and is the only fine art Smithsonian Affiliate between Orlando and Tampa" (Polk Museum of Art website). You can also request a tour from a Museum-trained docent tour guide, or join in on the monthly Curator Tour.

The museum features Modern and Contemporary Art; Art of the Ancient Americas; Asian Art; European Decorative Arts; and African Art. This is all in addition to the local art from students at Florida Southern College and various other local artists. Their exhibits change often, so make sure you checkout their website to see what they're currently featuring.

41. SUN 'N FUN

If you have a fan of aviation in your party, you may want to book a trip to Lakeland during the Sun 'n Fun convention. This weeklong expo is typically held in March or April and is nationally known for its aviation education and air shows. People really do fly in from all over the country to attend this event, and it's always a hit! The Blue Angels often perform as well, and this can be seen from a lot of places all over town. If you're planning to attend, it is suggested you make your accommodation reservations ahead of time as they do often fill up.

42. POLK THEATRE

If you love history and you love movies, the Polk Theatre is the place for you. This local historic masterpiece features Renaissance architecture and was built in 1928. It holds 1,400 people and is still operating. You can check online for a list of showings, but typically you'll find classics and family favorites on the screen here on the weekends. They also host events and live performances from ballets, symphonies, and more. The theatre makes for a unique viewing experience that is sure to enhance your memory of whatever it is you go to see. Sometimes I find it hard to focus on what I'm watching because I just want to look at the ornate artistry of the theatre itself.

43. SILVERMOON DRIVE-IN THEATRE

If you want to see what's new in movies, you can see it at Polk County's last remaining drive-in theatre, Silvermoon. With affordable snacks and the comfort of your own car, you'll wonder why you'd ever watch a movie another way. Another fact about this eclectic establishment: it was featured in the movie *The One and Only Ivan.*

During the COVID-19 shut down of 2020, Silvermoon was a savior to Lakeland residents. Not only were they able to stay open to show old movies, they also hosted events and concerts. We were able to go see Jimmy Allen from the comfort of our car. While they haven't hosted a concert in a while, it was still an amazing memory we got to share during a time when isolation was up and memory-making was low. It's definitely an important staple to Lakeland's locals.

44. DEFY LAKELAND

If you're looking for an indoor trampoline park to test out your skills or show up your kids, this one's for you! DEFY is located in North Lakeland and it's the perfect place to jump around and have some fun. My favorite area is the foam pit, but they also have trampoline walls, rock walls, and slam-style basketball hoops so no matter how short you are, you can dunk it. You do have to fill out a waiver before playing, and this can be found online ahead of time for your convenience.

45. BOK TOWER GARDENS

Located just outside the city in the town of Lake Wales, Bok Tower is a piece of tranquility. It's so unique it doesn't even feel like you're in Florida anymore (except that the weather is still perfect). This artistic bird sanctuary and contemplative garden gives guests the opportunity to relax and refresh in nature. Hang out on a blanket by the tower to hear it "sing". You'll have to go to know what we mean. You can also take a stroll around the Spanish mansion, "El Retiro" ("the retreat"). This 1930's mansion has tours available, or you can guide yourself through its stunning grounds.

If the point of your vacation is to relax, this is a great place to add to your itinerary. They have a cafe, the Blue Palmetto Cafe, onsite, so you don't even have to worry about packing food. After you're done, shop around the unique gift shop that's actually more of a greenhouse and bring a new plant baby home with you!

46. LEGOLAND

If a children's amusement park is what you seek, you will love Legoland. Located in the nearby town of Winter Haven, Legoland is made for kids ages 2-12 and is just a short drive away. Also in Legoland is the world's first Peppa Pig Theme Park and a water park, which is perfect for those hot Florida afternoons! Your kids will rave for days about this experience, and it's less than half the cost of other theme parks in the area. Ticket prices start at $84.99 and can be purchased ahead of time on their website. If you really want to go all-in, they have themed hotels on-site and package deals with food, tickets, and rooms. They also offer military discounts as a thank you to our service men, women, and their families for their sacrifice.

47. RP FUNDING CENTER

The RP Funding Center is an event center in the downtown Lakeland area that features all different types of entertainment. From sporting competition to musicals and ballets, the RP Funding Center does it all. Check out their website for upcoming events and tickets to make sure you snag yours before you get here!

48. LAKELAND MAGIC

The Lakeland Magic are the local NBA G league professional team. Their home games are held at the RP Funding Center and offer a fantastic option for the basketball lover in your life. They are owned by the nearby Orlando Magic, so even though they're not the "big time" team in Florida, the local games are always fun to attend. They give away thousands of prizes and have really great discounts for teachers and health care workers. They also celebrate diversity through their efforts to recognize minority groups during their months, such as the upcoming Hispanic Heritage Month game (November) and their Black History Month game (February). Tickets can be purchased ahead of time online or at the gate.

49. EXPLORATIONS V CHILDREN'S MUSEUM

Lakeland knows that children are the future, which is why the Exploration V Children's Museum exists to help kids nurture their curiosity. You may be wondering: what's the V for? It's the Roman Numeral for the number 5. This is symbolic of the 5 senses (smell, taste, touch, sight, and hear) which the museum engages through play throughout. This museum is located downtown around Munn Park and allows a fun, safe way for kids to play. It even has an orange juice factory! Local kids and tourist kids alike will be enthralled with their activities.

50. THE POOR PORKER

If you haven't ever gotten to experience beignets, head to the Poor Porker. This downtown, outdoor music venue features a small bar and yes, homemade, fresh beignets. Beignets are a French donut that is full of air and drenched in powdered sugar. If you still aren't convinced... just go anyway. They really are very good, and it's not something you can find just anywhere.

The eclectic outdoor space is one of a kind and is a great spot to wind down. They often feature live music from local performers, and the atmosphere is casual and relaxing. For parking, go across the street to the lot near Texas Cattle Company.

>TOURIST

TOP REASONS TO BOOK THIS TRIP:

Food: The food here is incredible. You won't find a better foodie spot in the state of Florida. Born and Bread Bakery is quickly becoming famous to foodies across the world, and the local staples like Black and Brew cafe, Cafe Zuppina, Red Door, and Nineteen61 allow visitors to taste cuisine from around the world without the big city waitlists and exclusivity. If you love food, you'll love Lakeland. I have extended family members who plan multiple yearly trips to visit and I know to make sure we have a Born and Bread pastry waiting for them when they get here because it's all they can think about while they're away.

Cost: The cost of staying and playing in Lakeland is much lower than that of the bigger cities. A stay at the local Hyatt Place will cost you around $90-$140 a night with no resort fees, while the Hyatt Place in Tampa ranges from $120-$240. Most resorts in Orlando come with steep resort fees added on, not to mention the higher prices of gas and parking, and the unavoidable trek through I-4 traffic. Polk County is also largely residential, so the sales tax on items you will buy here is much lower and comparable to other areas of the country. If you stay in Lakeland you can avoid most of the trouble of the overcrowded cities and still have access to all of the major theme parks, beaches, and events, which leads me to my next point.

Access to everything: Halfway between Orlando and Tampa means you have access to 2 major international airports (so book whichever is cheaper or fits your schedule best), Disney, Busch Gardens, Sea World, and Universal Studios, as well as the world famous Clearwater Beach. With Lakeland, you don't have to choose a beach stay or a theme park stay; you get to have both (or neither).

>TOURIST

DID YOU KNOW?

- Lakeland is the home of the famous supermarket chain Publix! You'll find one almost every mile or so, as well as its headquarters. Stop in for a chicken tender Pub sub for lunch!

- The famous movie *Edward Scissorhands* features the Southgate Publix neon sign. This sign is still operable, and often features lights that change with the season or local events. Drive by it at night for the full effect! This same plaza is used in the newer Disney movie, *The One and Only Ivan.*

- The city hires muralists to complete works of art all over in order to create an inclusive and beautiful place to live and travel to. You can find a map of the city murals on the popular Lakeland blog, Lakelandmom.com. I particularly love the Color Wall on Haus 820 located at 820 N. Massachusetts Ave, Lakeland, Florida. Bring a camera for this one because it's a popular place to do an Instagram-worthy photoshoot.

>TOURIST

OTHER RESOURCES:

Lakeland Parks and Recreation:
https://www.lakelandgov.net/departments/parks-recreation/

Downtown Lakeland Events:
https://downtownlkld.com

Local activities/events: https://laltoday.6amcity.com/

Map of the city murals:
https://lakelandmom.com/murals-in-lakeland-florida/

RP Funding Center events:
https://rpfundingcenter.com/images/flipbook/inc/html/34.html

Downtown parking info/maps:
https://www.lakelandgov.net/departments/public-works/parking/

The Squeeze evening hours map:

(courtesy of https://ridecitrus.com/about-us/the-squeeze/)

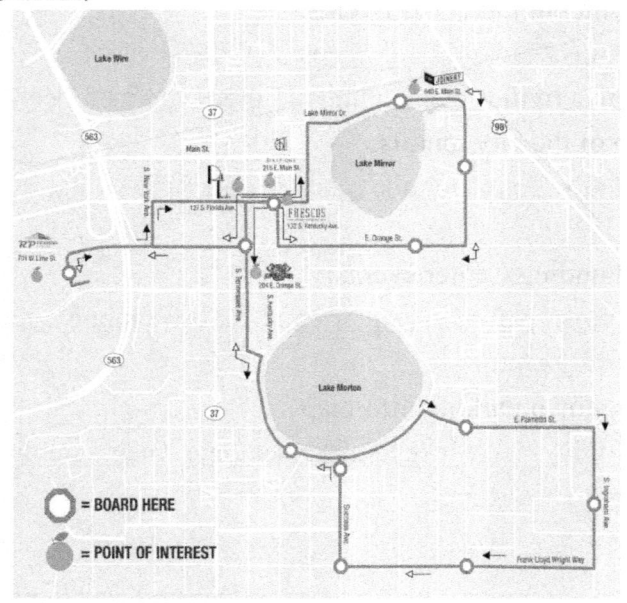

>TOURIST

TRIVIA

1) What two movies have been filmed in Lakeland, Florida?

2) What is the mascot for the championship high school football team in the city?

3) How many lakes are actually in Lakeland?

4) When was the first Detroit Tigers Spring Training?

5) How did Lakeland get its swans?

6) What 2 major cities is Lakeland between?

7) What major aviation event is held in Lakeland each year?

8) Who founded Publix in the city of Lakeland?

9) True or False: Elvis Presley once performed an iconic performance at the Polk Theatre.

10) How many colleges/universities are in Lakeland?

ANSWERS

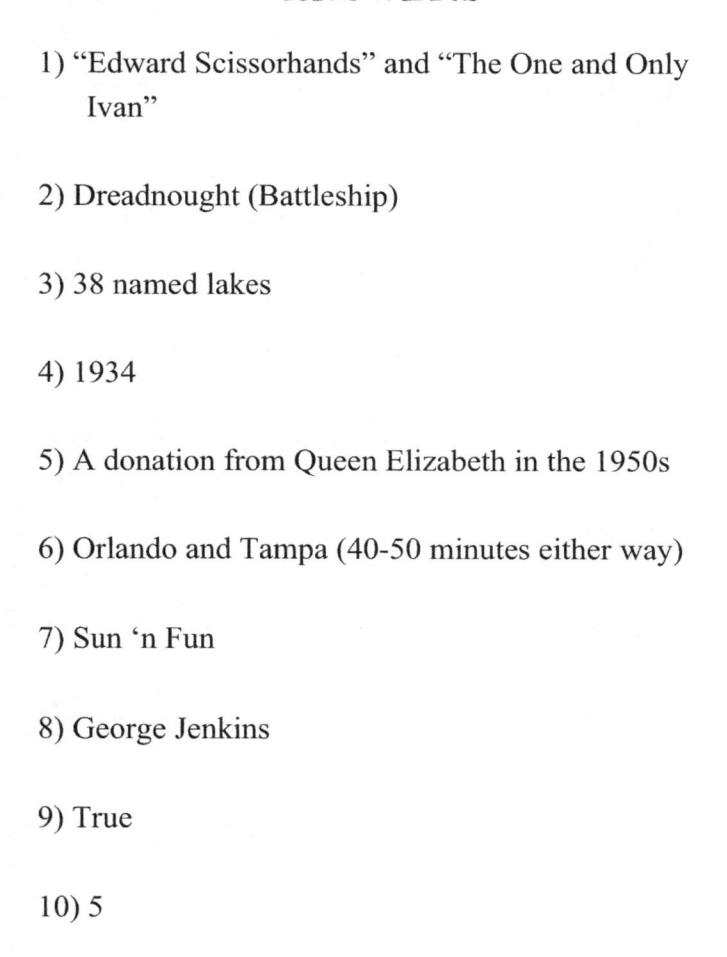

1) "Edward Scissorhands" and "The One and Only Ivan"

2) Dreadnought (Battleship)

3) 38 named lakes

4) 1934

5) A donation from Queen Elizabeth in the 1950s

6) Orlando and Tampa (40-50 minutes either way)

7) Sun 'n Fun

8) George Jenkins

9) True

10) 5

(Sources: LALtoday.com, citytowninfo.com, https://www.lakelandgov.net/, https://www.springtrainingonline.com)

>TOURIST

PACKING AND PLANNING TIPS

A Week before Leaving

- Arrange for someone to take care of pets and water plants.
- Email and Print important Documents.
- Get Visa and vaccines if needed.
- Check for travel warnings.
- Stop mail and newspaper.
- Notify Credit Card companies where you are going.
- Passports and photo identification is up to date.
- Pay bills.
- Copy important items and download travel Apps.
- Start collecting small bills for tips.
- Have post office hold mail while you are away.
- Check weather for the week.
- Car inspected, oil is changed, and tires have the correct pressure.
- Check airline luggage restrictions.
- Download Apps needed for your trip.

Right Before Leaving

- Contact bank and credit cards to tell them your location.
- Clean out refrigerator.
- Empty garbage cans.
- Lock windows.
- Make sure you have the proper identification with you.
- Bring cash for tips.
- Remember travel documents.
- Lock door behind you.
- Remember wallet.
- Unplug items in house and pack chargers.
- Change your thermostat settings.
- Charge electronics, and prepare camera memory cards.

>TOURIST

READ OTHER GREATER THAN A TOURIST BOOKS

Greater Than a Tourist- California: 50 Travel Tips from Locals

Greater Than a Tourist- Salem Massachusetts USA 50 Travel Tips from a Local by Danielle Lasher

Greater Than a Tourist United States: 50 Travel Tips from Locals

Greater Than a Tourist- St. Croix US Birgin Islands USA: 50 Travel Tips from a Local by Tracy Birdsall

Greater Than a Tourist- Montana: 50 Travel Tips from a Local by Laurie White

Children's Book: Charlie the Cavalier Travels the World by Lisa Rusczyk Ed. D.

> TOURIST

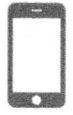

Follow us on Instagram for beautiful travel images:
http://Instagram.com/GreaterThanATourist

Follow *Greater Than a Tourist* on Amazon.

CZYKPublishing.com

> TOURIST

At *Greater Than a Tourist*, we love to share travel tips with you. How did we do? What guidance do you have for how we can give you better advice for your next trip? Please send your feedback to GreaterThanaTourist@gmail.com as we continue to improve the series. We appreciate your constructive feedback. Thank you.

>TOURIST

METRIC CONVERSIONS

TEMPERATURE

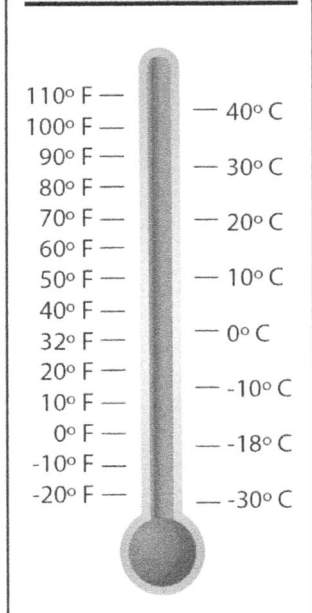

110° F — — 40° C
100° F —
90° F — — 30° C
80° F —
70° F — — 20° C
60° F —
50° F — — 10° C
40° F —
32° F — — 0° C
20° F —
10° F — — -10° C
0° F —
-10° F — — -18° C
-20° F — — -30° C

To convert F to C:
Subtract 32, and then multiply by 5/9 or .5555.

To Convert C to F:
Multiply by 1.8 and then add 32.

32F = 0C

LIQUID VOLUME

To Convert:...................Multiply by
U.S. Gallons to Liters................ 3.8
U.S. Liters to Gallons 26
Imperial Gallons to U.S. Gallons 1.2
Imperial Gallons to Liters....... 4.55
Liters to Imperial Gallons 22
1 Liter = .26 U.S. Gallon
1 U.S. Gallon = 3.8 Liters

DISTANCE

To convert ....Multiply by
Inches to Centimeters 2.54
Centimeters to Inches 39
Feet to Meters....................... .3
Meters to Feet 3.28
Yards to Meters 91
Meters to Yards 1.09
Miles to Kilometers 1.61
Kilometers to Miles............ .62
1 Mile = 1.6 km
1 km = .62 Miles

WEIGHT

1 Ounce = .28 Grams
1 Pound = .4555 Kilograms
1 Gram = .04 Ounce
1 Kilogram = 2.2 Pounds

>TOURIST

TRAVEL QUESTIONS

- Do you bring presents home to family or friends after a vacation?
- Do you get motion sick?
- Do you have a favorite billboard?
- Do you know what to do if there is a flat tire?
- Do you like a sun roof open?
- Do you like to eat in the car?
- Do you like to wear sun glasses in the car?
- Do you like toppings on your ice cream?
- Do you use public bathrooms?
- Did you bring a cell phone and does it have power?
- Do you have a form of identification with you?
- Have you ever been pulled over by a cop?
- Have you ever given money to a stranger on a road trip?
- Have you ever taken a road trip with animals?
- Have you ever gone on a vacation alone?
- Have you ever run out of gas?

- If you could move to any place in the world, where would it be?
- If you could travel anywhere in the world, where would you travel?
- If you could travel in any vehicle, which one would it be?
- If you had three things to wish for from a magic genie, what would they be?
- If you have a driver's license, how many times did it take you to pass the test?
- What are you the most afraid of on vacation?
- What do you want to get away from the most when you are on vacation?
- What foods smell bad to you?
- What item do you bring on ever trip with you away from home?
- What makes you sleepy?
- What song would you love to hear on the radio when you're cruising on the highway?
- What travel job would you want the least?
- What will you miss most while you are away from home?
- What is something you always wanted to try?

>TOURIST

- What is the best road side attraction that you ever saw?
- What is the farthest distance you ever biked?
- What is the farthest distance you ever walked?
- What is the weirdest thing you needed to buy while on vacation?
- What is your favorite candy?
- What is your favorite color car?
- What is your favorite family vacation?
- What is your favorite food?
- What is your favorite gas station drink or food?
- What is your favorite license plate design?
- What is your favorite restaurant?
- What is your favorite smell?
- What is your favorite song?
- What is your favorite sound that nature makes?
- What is your favorite thing to bring home from a vacation?
- What is your favorite vacation with friends?
- What is your favorite way to relax?
- Where is the farthest place you ever traveled in a car?

- Where is the farthest place you ever went North, South, East and West?
- Where is your favorite place in the world?
- Who is your favorite singer?
- Who taught you how to drive?
- Who will you miss the most while you are away?
- Who if the first person you will contact when you get to your destination?
- Who brought you on your first vacation?
- Who likes to travel the most in your life?
- Would you rather be hot or cold?
- Would you rather drive above, below, or at the speed limited?
- Would you rather drive on a highway or a back road?
- Would you rather go on a train or a boat?
- Would you rather go to the beach or the woods?

>TOURIST

TRAVEL BUCKET LIST

1.

2.

3.

4.

5.

6.

7.

8.

9.

10.

>TOURIST

NOTES

Made in the USA
Monee, IL
11 September 2022